# *Ice sports*

This book describes the world of ice skating from the grace and beauty of the figure skaters to the fast, thrilling sport of ice hockey. If you can skate already, or if you want to learn, there are many exciting colour photographs and useful tips to help you along the way.

InterSport

# Ice Sports

**Clive Millard and Susan Crimp**

**Colour photographs by All-Sport Limited**

Wayland / Silver Burdett

# InterSport

The world of international sport seen through the cameras of some of the world's greatest sports photographers, showing in action both children and the stars they admire.

| | |
|---|---|
| Basketball | On Horseback |
| Cycling | Snow Sports |
| Golf | Soccer |
| Gymnastics | Swimming and Diving |
| Ice Sports | Tennis |
| Motorcycling | Track and Field |

Frontispiece: **In flight** – Karena Richardson of Great Britain puts on a graceful, airborne display.

First published in 1980 by Wayland Publishers Limited
49 Lansdowne Place, Hove, East Sussex BN3 1HF, England

ISBN 0 85340 788 6

Published in the United States by Silver Burdett Company, Morristown, New Jersey
1980 Printing
ISBN 0–382 06428–3

Phototypeset by Trident Graphics Limited, Reigate, Surrey
Printed in Italy by G. Canale & C.S.p.A., Turin

# Contents

# Beginnings

Skating has existed in one form or another for thousands of years. Our hungry ancestors would slide across the ice on pieces of wood or blades carved from animal bones in search of food.

Sliding across ice on pieces of wood is, of course, far removed from the skating of today. Credit for modern-day skating must be given to the Dutch. While James, Duke of York, was spending his exile in Holland in the seventeenth century, he became aware of this recreational pastime. On his return to England, he introduced the sport to his subjects and, since then, skating has grown in popularity all over the world. In Britain alone, skating is second only to professional football in terms of the television audiences it attracts.

Skating provides the basis for many ice sports – figure, free, dance, pair and speed skating, and ice hockey – so before you can begin to participate in any of these, it is necessary to get a basic idea of skating itself.

The number of ice rinks is definitely on the increase, and it is hoped that by the end of

**Even the great must practice** – Robin Cousins of Great Britain, Olympic and European Figure Skating Champion, is considered 'weak' in his compulsory figures. So, even a World Champion must still devote many hours a day in search of perfection!

the decade everyone will have rinks within easy reach of home.

Since the Second World War, ice rinks have appeared all over the world, and all of these provide the basic facilities for every beginner – good ice, and skates which you can hire at very reasonable prices. All you have to do is to dress up in loose, warm clothing and have a sense of adventure.

Most people's natural reaction when they step on to the ice for the first time is to walk. However, the essence of skating is gliding. If you have already visited an ice rink you will probably have seen many beginners losing their balance and falling. The reason for this is a very simple one – their knees are stiff. You should always remember to bend your knees and to balance so that the whole of your body weight is transferred on to the thigh of the leg you are skating with. Once you learn to control your thigh, that control will extend to your feet automatically.

After a few visits to the rink you will know for yourself whether you want to continue. If you do, it is best at this stage to talk to a professional trainer. All rinks have them, and even though individual lessons are expensive, most rinks run group classes which are often inexpensive.

**Early promise** – This young East German skater shows a balance, grace and self-confidence that belies her tender years.

# The variety of ice sports

There are many different kinds of ice sports. Often the only things they have in common are the ice on which they take place and the skates which the sportsmen wear. But the skates themselves are quite different for each sport.

It is quite possible that you may be particularly attracted to one ice sport while remaining unaware of the opportunities that the others can offer. So, in the next six sections we will look at figure, free, dance, pair and speed skating, and ice hockey, outlining the principles and, in some cases, the origins behind them.

If you ask any of the champions the reasons for their success, they will probably tell you that although physical ability counts for a great deal, the right mental attitude is the most important quality.

So now it is up to you to take your pick, and choose the ice sport which, apart from giving you immense excitement and satisfaction, may even make you a star of the ice!

**Viewing with a new interest** – Before the Lake Placid Olympics in 1980, speed skating was not one of the most popular spectator sports. All this was changed by the exploits of Eric Heiden of the U.S.A. – who won all five gold medals in the men's events – thrilling huge audiences at the stadium, and millions of television viewers throughout the world.

**Elegance on ice**
Moiseeva and Minnenkov of the U.S.S.R. show all the style that makes ice dancing such a graceful sport. Immaculately dressed ice dancers can perform many of the ballroom dances that would tangle you and me on the dance floor – the Viennese waltz, the quickstep, the paso doble, the tango and the rumba.

# Figure skating

**Tracing a fine line** – Skates used for figures have a single steel blade about 3 mm wide, hollow-ground at the bottom to give two skating edges, and figures are skated on the inside or outside edge.

One of the most widely known ice sports is figure skating. It is fitting that we should look at this sport first, since figure skating is the starting point for most ice sportsmen.

Figure skating demands the ability to exactly trace out on the ice the forty-one compulsory or 'school' figures. For the beginner, the first step is learning to trace circles on the ice. This may sound rather complicated to you now, but once you have studied a skater tracing figures, it will begin to seem very easy. When you watch figure skating on the television, or at a skating championship, it may seem rather tedious. But, to the skaters, there is nothing more rewarding than being able to perform the exact figure where and when they want it on the ice.

There are two types of figure skating: the English style (the oldest) and International figure skating. The English style, which dates back to pre-Victorian times, is far less extravagant and dramatic than the newer style, but it tends to offer more opportunities for team and individual skating. Nowadays, it is only practised at very few rinks

**Quite simply breathtaking** – It seems hardly credible, but Lisa Marie Allen of the U.S.A. completed this jump with grace, and made a perfect landing!

**In an expressive spin** Dorothy Hamill of the U.S.A. shows the ability to express herself, and interpret the music, whilst in the middle of a difficult spin (right).

1975 WORLD
FIGURE SKATING
CHAMPIONSHIPS
Krakus
CANNED MEAT FROM

however, and you may find difficulty in participating.

International figure skating is probably quite familiar to you already as it accounts for the first third of all the major ice skating championships, and commands thirty per cent of the competitors' total marks.

The clothing you wear for figure skating is largely a matter of personal choice. There are, however, special figure skating boots, and if you plan to take this sport seriously, it is well worth investing in a pair. Figure skating boots have a blade which normally measures 3 millimetres in width, and is slightly curved from head to toe. The toe rake at the front of the blade looks rather like teeth, and is there to assist with the jumps, spins and pivots.

Figure skating is an extremely sociable sport and can be enjoyed by all ages. But it is, of course, important for those wishing to become as proficient as East Germany's Jan Hoffman, to start young and receive regular professional tuition. At international level a professional coach is absolutely essential.

**Under eagle eyes** – During the compulsory figures section, a maximum of nine judges and one referee watch the competitors trace their figures.

# Free skating

Free skating is probably the most well-known and best-loved ice sport among spectators. And, for you as a skater, it creates so many opportunities to do anything you want.

Free skating consists of many jumps and spins which, for the novice, can prove as difficult as the names of them. It must be remembered though, that anything which is done well is largely the result of years of hard work.

One of the most spectacular free skaters is Switzerland's Denise Biellmann. Her long free skating programmes always give immense pleasure to spectators and fellow competitors alike. Denise spins, jumps and pivots on her skates as easily as we walk on land. She shows great balance and beauty, and certainly sets a wonderful example for young free skaters.

Free skating is fun and fascinating because there are no limitations. It is a combination of the skater's individuality and freedom of movement to music which makes free skating such a pleasure for television viewers all over the world.

**Reaching dizzy heights** – Robin Cousins of Great Britain shows the incredible height he achieves during his jumps.

For those of you who take up free skating, there is immense pleasure in store and a great opportunity to use your imagination. The skater can choose his or her own music, and often the costumes and style of programme as well.

If you enjoy music, and indeed if you have a feel for it, then free skating is definitely the ice sport for you. In your skating programme, you can use any type of music – modern, classical, disco – so you can skate in your own style to your favourite piece of music.

Choosing music is no easy task, but it is great fun and there's a vast amount to choose from. The most important thing is that you must like the music, because you will have to listen to it many, many times, both at home and at rehearsals. And when you start winning medals, you will hear it on the television too!

Free skating allows you to exhibit your best moves in whatever order you like, to the music of your choice. So if you like being your own master and having no limitations or restrictions, then you couldn't do better than to take up free skating. Get in touch with a trainer – he or she will be able to advise you better than anyone else.

**At full stretch** – This youngster has not yet got the grace and style of Linda Fratianne . . . yet she certainly lacks nothing in determination!

**The ultimate spin** – Denise Biellmann of Switzerland is arguably the finest women's free skater in the world. Here she demonstrates the extraordinary 'Biellmann Spin'.

# Dance

Ice dancing is enjoyed by both young and old, and it is certainly a sport for all the family for it has a great social side to it.

Ice dancing can be compared to ballroom dancing, but the main difference between them is quite simply the ice which slides beneath the dancers' feet and allows greater speed. Ice dancers enjoy an advantage over other ice sportsmen because most rinks clear the ice during sessions for the dancers themselves.

Just like ballroom dancing, ice dancing has its compulsory dances such as the waltz and the polka. There is also an original set pattern dance in championships. This comprises a dance invented by the couple, and usually proves to be very interesting for the skaters because they are allowed to create a totally new dance routine.

Ice dancing is a very beautiful sport, both for the spectator and for the dancer. It is also a very precise sport, and demands a lot of grace on the ice dancer's part.

As an ice dancer, you will enjoy the benefit of your partner's advice and encouragement,

**Exuberance** – A good pair skating programme includes many different moods and musical themes. Here Linichuk and Karponosov of the U.S.S.R. interpret some light-hearted music.

**Strength, balance and grace** – O'Conner and Millns of the U.S.A. demonstrate that pair skating of any description involves being perfectly in tune with your partner.

and the beauty of working in complete harmony with another person. As in pair skating, you can build up a great sense of teamwork between yourself and your partner.

Britain has produced many ice dance

**A touch of drama** – Henrietta Frosch and Christian Steiner of Germany 'perform' on the ice in much the same way as actors perform on the stage.

champions, but probably the two best-known and best-loved ice dancers of recent years have been the Russian couple, Gennadi Karponosov and Natalia Linichuk.

There are lots of opportunities to take up ice dancing, and you can start at virtually any age. And it is not as disheartening for the beginner as some of the more disciplined ice sports can be, because progress is often very quick. You will be most surprised at how impressive your dancing looks even after a few lessons.

# Pair skating

**United flamboyance** – Tai Babilonia and Randy Gardner of the U.S.A. are the 'heirs apparent' to Rodnina and Zaitsev.

Of all the ice sports, pair skating is one of the most attractive and pleasing to the eye. It is basically a form of free skating in which two people participate, and involves absolute accuracy, precision and harmony between the two skaters.

The basis of pair skating is teamwork, and the man and woman together skate a series of jumps, steps, spins and lifts to music.

Pair skating is, however, a very difficult sport, in the sense that you not only have to be able to skate excellently yourself, but you have to adapt your style of skating to the style of your partner.

Probably the pair skaters who are largely responsible for the growing popularity of the sport in recent years, are Irina Rodrina, the Ice Queen from Moscow, and her husband, Alexander Zaitsev.

This couple has dominated pair skating for many years, and their unique run of successes was only interrupted once when Irina took a rest following the birth of their son, Sacha.

Since their comeback, they have had

**Perfect harmony** – Irina Rodnina and Alexander Zaitsev are the greatest pair skaters in the world. They are justly famous for their united, harmonious performances.

constant success. At Gothenburg, Sweden, in January 1980, they regained their European title, making a total of eleven European gold medals for Irina and seven for Alexander. This was followed in February 1980 by Irina's third Olympic gold medal at the Lake Placid Winter Olympics.

You will, no doubt, remember her emotional tears at Lake Placid, when she stood on the podium and collected her medal, a sight which touched so many spectators and television viewers the world over.

For those of you who have been inspired by Irina and Alexander's marvellous achievements, it is advisable to reach a high standard of individual free skating first. Then you can join up with a partner to share your groundwork and create new ideas.

**In good hands** – Faith in your partner's ability is essential to the pair skater, as some movements are not only spectacular but also dangerous. The lifts demand great strength and balance. Lifting is permitted only with the hands, and the lifting arm must be fully extended.

USA

# Speed skating

**Truly the golden boy** – Eric Heiden of the U.S.A. can justly be called one of the most amazing athletes in the world. He won every medal in the men's speed skating at the Lake Placid Olympics, from 500 m to 10,000 m.

Speed skating is the oldest of the ice sports, and records have been found of the sport taking place way back in the thirteenth century.

Speed skating today is generally an outdoor sport because of the sheer distance required. However, there are some indoor tracks for short events.

Speed skating is more popular in countries with colder climates, although major championships are often held on refrigerated ice.

Distances of races vary from 500 metres to over 10,000 metres, but for women's races, the maximum is generally 5000 metres.

Champion speed skaters are the fastest self-propelled humans and can achieve, on average, a good speed of 53 km/h (33 mph). Because of this, proper clothing is essential.

Usually, this consists of woollen leggings over a one-piece nylon suit, sweater, gloves and a warm hood. The skates, too, are very different from those used for other ice sports. They are very low-heeled and are quite similar to a shoe in appearance.

Their design is based on the principles of strength and lightness. The blades of speed

DESCENTE

**An impressive stage** – Two skaters take a bend before 'crossing' in the straight. Skaters must change lanes each time they reach the crossing straight, and it is the responsibility of the skater leaving the inner lane to avoid any collision.

**Skates poised** – Bjoers-Eva Jensen of Norway, about to start a women's 3000 m race. Speed skates have much longer blades than those worn by figure skaters (left).

skates are very long, 42 cm on average, and are approximately 1 mm thick.

Speed skating has always been very much a participator's sport, but at the 1980 Olympics at Lake Placid, more spectators began to take an interest when the event seemed like something taken from a fairytale. The reason behind this was the American speed skater, Eric Heiden, who won five Olympic gold medals in two weeks.

Speed skating can be great fun, and even if

you live in an area where the climate is not suited to outdoor skating, many rinks provide indoor facilities, so it is well worth investigating.

If you enjoy speed and exhilaration, then this ice sport is definitely the one for you. As a speed skater, you will be travelling at speeds that you never thought were possible on foot.

Another brilliant feature of speed skating is the racing aspect, not only against other skaters but more excitingly against the clock. So even after the race you will still have the suspense and excitement left in finding out your time.

Eric Heiden, the world's champion speed skater, has made some remarkable achievements in this sport, but, with lots of practice, there is no reason why you cannot equal him. Because of the shortage of speed skaters in most countries, you will find lots of enthusiastic people encouraging your progress – so why not give it a try?

**'Going for broke'** – Sheila Young of the U.S.A. holds nothing back as she glides round the sometimes treacherous bend of a circuit.

# Ice hockey

The origins of the sport of ice hockey are quite obscure, but it is thought to have been derived from field hockey, lacrosse and the old English game of bandy.

Rules of play were established by R. F. Smith of Montreal in 1879, and the first game was played between two teams from McGill University in Montreal.

Soon the game spread to other parts of Canada, the U.S.A. and then to Europe. Ice hockey is now the national sport in many European countries, the U.S.A. and Canada.

Nowadays, ice hockey is played with six players from each side on the ice; the goalminder, two defencemen and three forwards. There are also several other players which each team coach can use by substituting them for players on the ice.

If you have watched a game of ice hockey on the television you will know that it is quite a tough sport. Because of this, the players wear protective clothing in case they are hit by competitors' sticks or the puck (the small vulcanized rubber disc with which the game is played). Ice hockey boots are also

**They shall not pass** – This young goalminder appears determined to defend his goal at all costs.

**All the Poles** – The whole 'on-ice' Polish team of six can be seen in this picture of a face-off taken during a game against the U.S.S.R. (right).

FINLAND
8
JOHNSON
10
KOSKINEN
21
3
17

**About to clear** – This Russian will waste no time in clearing the puck away from the 'danger zone' in front of his own goal.

well padded at the toe and the heel. The goalminders are especially well protected – they wear leg-guards, a crash helmet and, quite frequently, a face mask.

The game begins with a face-off. The referee drops the puck between the two opposing centres, who stand facing each other in the middle of the rink. Generally there are not many stoppages since the boards at the side of the rink keep the puck in play. When the game is stopped because of offside, or if the puck is shot out of the rink

**The face-off** – The referee in this game between the U.S.A. and Finland is about to drop the puck between the sticks of the two facing players (left).

or trapped against the boards, play is restarted with another face-off.

Each game consists of three twenty-minute periods, with a ten-minute intermission between periods. If the score is tied, a 'sudden-death' ten-minute overtime is sometimes played and the first team to score wins the game.

The game is played at a very fast pace and involves a series of short dashes. Rapid starting and stopping, turning, dodging and weaving are all part of the player's routine and these techniques must be learned before

**Goalmouth scuffle** – Unlike soccer and field hockey, play in ice hockey takes place in the area behind each goal. A goalminder sometimes needs eyes in the back of his head if he is to follow the play at all times!

**All eyes on the puck** – The Canadian goalminder dives full length in an attempt to foil two Russian forwards.

you can pick up a stick and begin to play.

If you want to become an ice hockey player you must first learn the art of good hockey skating. You must then learn how to handle the stick. Skaters use various methods to control the puck. Some skate with it close in front of them and others keep it at stick's length, flicking it from side to side when they approach an opponent. The exact shape of the stick you will use will depend upon which way you like to 'carry the puck'.

But acquiring the skill of stick-handling is not enough. You must also know how to take

**In close attendance** – A Polish player attempts to pass the puck before 'being closed in on' by three Russians.

the puck away from an opponent. This can be done either by checking with the stick or by body checking, but you have to be careful not to foul your opponent at the same time.

A good ice hockey player never needs to look at his feet, his stick or the puck. Skating and controlling the puck have become second nature, and he can keep his eyes on his opponents and team-mates.

It is important to remember that ice hockey is a team game. A single-handed rush towards the goal is rarely successful – goals

**On the boards** – This Canadian player (in red) seems to have come off worst during this crunching collision on the boards. Ice hockey is a very physical game and a certain amount of 'checking' is permitted – so long as the referee does not view it as 'dangerous'.

are normally scored after a complex pattern of passes and interceptions.

Even if you have beaten the opposing defencemen, you still have to force the puck past the goalminder. This is not as easy as it may sound, especially if the person facing you is the great Russian goalie, Tretyak. The most vulnerable parts of the goal are the upper and lower corners. But you need to be a very skilful shooter to hit these spots, and a very good goalminder to block them.

Ice hockey is played by both professionals

**Fully protected** – and he needs to be! The puck about to clatter into the guard in front of Tretyak's face is made of vulcanized rubber, and very, very hard! It sometimes travels at over 100 mph.

**The size of the target** – An ice hockey goal is 1.22 m (4 ft) high and 1.83 m (6 ft) wide. It probably seems twice as big to this grounded West German goalminder and half the size to the American attacker about to shoot! (left).

and amateurs, and it is so popular in North America that there are several professional leagues. The number of amateur teams is also increasing and, in the U.S.A. alone, more than a million youngsters have taken up the sport.

In professional ice hockey in North America, the highest prize is the Stanley Cup, and the team which wins it is regarded as the year's champion team.

The first Olympic Games which included

KOHO

**It's there!** – Joy for the Russians, despair for the Poles.

NORTHLAND
RISTOFF
11
HARRINGTON
28
WELLS
15

ice hockey were held in Antwerp, Belgium in 1920. The Canadians won the tournament and continued to do so until Great Britain took the gold medal in 1936 in Garmisch, West Germany. After the war, the Canadians had another run of supremacy until the Russians won in 1956. The U.S.A. finally achieved victory in the 1960 Olympics, since when, the U.S.S.R. have completely dominated the Olympic ice hockey tournaments.

But, at the 1980 Winter Olympics, the tables were turned and the host nation, the U.S.A., took their first ice hockey gold medal since 1960. Steve Cristoff was undoubtedly the man of the final match, and the American goalminder Craig was the star of the tournament. The American victory was greeted with jubilation throughout the country and the ice hockey team were entertained at the White House by President Carter.

Ice hockey is, without doubt, one of the most popular sports at the Winter Olympics. The goal-scoring and the speed of play make it very spectacular to watch. There is probably only one thing more exciting than watching a fast, action-packed game, and that is playing in one. So if you want to give it a try, find a rink where the sport is played, go along there and see if you can get a game.

**American jubilation** – The U.S.A. team celebrate after defeating the U.S.S.R. during the 1980 Winter Olympics.

# Stars of the ice

Each ice sport, like all other sports, produces its champions. They may spring from an ice hockey team, or from dance, or pair skating couples. Or they make their way individually through figure, free or speed skating. Whatever their discipline, their reasons for success are the same – dedication, ambition and determination.

You may feel that an Olympic gold medal is far beyond your capability. However, let us now look at one man and one woman who thought just like you. As you will see, they have proved themselves, and others, wrong.

## *Robin Cousins*

In recent years, Robin Cousins has certainly been the golden boy of skating from the British point-of-view and, like Britain's John Curry, took the European and Olympic gold medals in the same year (although Curry added the World Championships gold medal to his tally). Because of this, Robin Cousins has become a household name and an international skating celebrity.

Robin, who was born in Bristol, began

**Unbeatable brother, brilliant sister** – Eric and Beth Heiden are both world-class speed skaters. Eric is *the* best, Beth, very much one of the best.

skating purely by chance, whilst on holiday with his parents and two older brothers in Bournemouth. Robin's father decided to take the two older boys to play golf but Robin, who was too young to join in, stayed with his mother on the beach.

As the holidaymakers began to gather, Robin and his mother decided to wander around the town to avoid the crowd. On coming across an ice rink they decided they would go in to cool down. Once on the ice Robin enjoyed every moment and had never experienced so much fun from anything before.

For the rest of the holiday the memory of the Bournemouth ice rink remained with Robin, and on his return to Bristol he knew he had to skate again. At the age of nine Robin embarked on a 'Learn to Skate Course' and began to take his skating seriously right from the very first lesson. For seven and a half years he enjoyed the encouragement and tuition of his coach Pam Davis in Bristol.

Pam then advised Robin to go to London to receive the international experience which she could not offer him. He took her advice and lived in a London bedsit while he was coached at Queen's Ice Rink in the heart of London by Gladys Hogg.

Filled with ambition and determination, Robin would arrive at Queen's at 6.00 a.m. every day, skate until lunchtime, then walk round the corner to do his part-time job in a department store. He would then return to Queen's in the evening for further practice.

It is not surprising that after all this hard work Robin's rewards began to come. Carlo Fassi, one of the world's finest coaches, spotted Robin's potential. He invited Robin to join him and his wife, Christa, at their rink in Denver, Colorado.

Since that time Robin has never looked back, and the hard struggle in his early years has been highly compensated by the gold medals and cups which he has won as a result of his work and determination.

## *Linda Fratianne*

Linda Fratianne is America's number one skater and is one of the most popular skaters

**Britain's pride** – Robin Cousins of Britain came within a whisker of emulating the achievement of John Curry, his fellow countryman, who won the Olympic, World and European titles during a single year. Cousins had to satisfy himself with an Olympic gold, a European gold and a World silver medal!

on the ice today. Her skating performances are a combination of excellence and grace. Linda was born on August 2nd, 1960, in California, U.S.A.

Like Robin Cousins, Linda began skating at the age of nine, but this is purely coincidental and if you are ten years or older, do not think that you can never become a champion. Both Linda and Robin will tell you that champions become champions through determination.

Linda took to the ice very well and was quick in reaching a high standard. At the age of twelve she was awarded the United States Skating Association's gold medal, an award rarely given to people of such a young age.

In 1977, Linda won the National Skating Championships, and in a country as vast as the United States, this was quite an achievement, and in the same year she took the gold medal in Tokyo.

The following year, 1978, Linda came second in the World Championships despite being placed first in the short and long free skating programmes.

At the 1980 Winter Olympics in Lake Placid, she finished disappointingly with a silver medal.

But Linda is very young and she can only get better. Much of her success has been the result of the hard work and enthusiasm provided by her coach, Frank Carroll.

**America's favourite daughter** – Linda Fratianne only narrowly missed winning the figure skating gold medal during the Lake Placid Olympics in 1980.

# Championships

Probably the most important championships as far as ice sportsmen are concerned are the Winter Olympics. They are the only championships where figure, free, pair, dance and speed skating take place simultaneously.

Figure skating, for both men and women, had already established itself as a major Olympic sport in 1908, but it was not until ice hockey was introduced to the Games in 1920, that pressure was applied for a separate Olympic Games for winter sports. Finally the Winter Olympics were granted recognition and became a separate event in 1924.

Ice hockey today forms a very exciting event in every Winter Olympics and the spectators have the opportunity to watch a total of seventy-two games.

Figure skating is also very popular and consists of three sections, the compulsory figures, the short programme and, everyone's favourite, the long free skating programme. For the long programme each skater is allowed five minutes to skate in any style, to the music of their choice.

**Fully extended** – The Canadian goalminder stretches forth his padded leg in an attempt to block the path to goal.

CCCP
13
WATTERS
5
CCM

**Practised precision** – This sort of perfection is only achieved through practice, practice . . . and more practice!

Speed skating, as an Olympic sport, has several variations; each event varies in length and time. Because of this, speed skating usually accounts for a large part of the Olympic timetable.

Apart from the Winter Olympics, the highlights of every skater's career are the European and World Figure Skating Championships. These are structured in the same way as the Winter Olympics, but they do not include speed skating. As in the Olympics, the figure skating consists of three events, the compulsory figures, the short programme of two minutes, and the long programme of four minutes for the ladies and five minutes for the men.

For the pairs there are two sections: the short programme and the free skating. Like the figure skaters, the dancers compete in three sections. They start with two compulsory dances and then a compulsory dance and original set pattern. There is also a final free skating section to decide the winner.

In addition to the European and World Championships, there are many national championships at both junior and senior levels. Also, in recent years sponsors have encouraged some of the world's best skaters to perform in exhibitions. These have proved so popular that some have become annual events. So there are many opportunities open to you both as a skater and as a spectator.

**The sweet, sweet, smell of success** – Robin Cousins is undoubtedly the greatest free skater in the world today – but who will step into his skates?

# Index